Animal Teams

# Bee Colonies

by Trudy Becker

FOCUS READERS

BEACON

www.focusreaders.com



Focus Readers is distributed by North Star Editions:
sales@northstareditions.com | 888-417-0195

Produced for Focus Readers by Red Line Editorial.

Photographs ©: Shutterstock Images, cover, 1, 4, 7, 8, 11, 12, 14–15, 16, 19, 21, 22, 25, 26, 29

**Library of Congress Cataloging-in-Publication Data**
Names: Becker, Trudy, author.
Title: Bee colonies / by Trudy Becker.
Description: Mendota Heights, MN: Focus Readers, [2025] | Series: Animal teams | Includes index. | Audience: Grades 2-3
Identifiers: LCCN 2023053427 (print) | LCCN 2023053428 (ebook) | ISBN 9798889981909 (hardcover) | ISBN 9798889982463 (paperback) | ISBN 9798889983552 (pdf) | ISBN 9798889983026 (ebook)
Subjects: LCSH: Bees--Juvenile literature | Bees--Behavior--Juvenile literature | Bees--Life cycles--Juvenile literature
Classification: LCC QL565.2 .B395 2025 (print) | LCC QL565.2 (ebook) | DDC 595.79/9--dc23/eng/20231220
LC record available at https://lccn.loc.gov/2023053427
LC ebook record available at https://lccn.loc.gov/2023053428

Printed in the United States of America
Mankato, MN
082024

## About the Author

Trudy Becker lives in Minneapolis, Minnesota. She likes exploring new places and loves anything involving books.

# Table of Contents

Chapter 1

# Pollen for All

It is springtime. Several bees zoom through the warm air. They fly from flower to flower. The bees are collecting **pollen**. When the bees have enough pollen, they go back to the nest.

**Bees can collect pollen from many different types of flowers.**

Thousands of other bees wait there. They take the pollen. They store it safely in the nest. And they use it to feed the bee **larvae**. The pollen helps the larvae grow.

But the task is not done with one trip. The nest needs more pollen. So, the bees fly back out

When bees collect pollen, they spread material between flowers. That helps flowers **reproduce**.

**A nest of honeybees can collect more than 125 pounds (57 kg) of pollen per year.**

again. They visit more flowers. They will get enough pollen for the whole nest. The bees work hard for the group.

Chapter 2

# What Is a Colony?

There are many different kinds of bees. Most types live alone. Those include leafcutter bees and carpenter bees. But some bees are **social** animals. They live together in **colonies**.

**An average honeybee hive is nearly 2 feet (0.6 m) tall.**

The bees do many tasks to help their colonies survive. Each bee has its own job. But the actions of each bee help support the group. Together, the whole colony works as one unit.

There are three main types of bees in a colony. Each type has a different role. The most important bee is the queen. A nest usually has just one queen. Her job is to lay eggs. That helps the colony survive. If she lays enough eggs,

**A queen bee (center) has shorter wings and a more pointed back end than other bees.**

the colony will not die out. A queen can lay more than one million eggs in her lifetime.

**A drone bee (right) is usually larger than a worker bee.**

Another type of bee is a drone. Every drone is male. A colony might have a few hundred of them. Drones have only one job. They **mate** with the queen. Then they die.

The largest group in a colony is the worker bee. Each colony has thousands of workers. These bees are all female. Worker bees do many difficult jobs. They help the colony stay clean, safe, and fed.

When a queen dies, some workers lay a few special eggs. One hatches and kills the others. She becomes the new queen.

THAT'S AMAZING!

# Bee Communication

For colonies to work smoothly, bees need to communicate. Bees release **pheromones**. These chemicals have scents. The scents share meanings to other bees. Bees can show that there is food nearby. Or they can show that there is danger.

Bees also use movement to communicate. They shake their bodies. Other bees see these movements. Then, they know what to do. They can help the colony.

**Bees release pheromones from glands on their faces.**

Chapter 3

# Work in the Nest

Worker bees do many jobs around the nest. Workers are born in cells. When they hatch, their first jobs happen there. The workers start cleaning up their cells. They prepare the cells for the queen.

**After hatching, bees chew their way out of their cells.**

She will lay new eggs there. That way, the cycle of life can continue.

As worker bees get older, they start new tasks. The next jobs are taking care of larvae and young bees. The queen lays those eggs for the colony. But the workers in the colony care for the young. For instance, the workers bring food to

Worker bees feed young bees a substance called royal jelly.

**Most honeybees spend approximately five days as larvae.**

them. They help the young survive until they are older.

Worker bees do other tasks in the nest, too. For example, they make sure the nest doesn't get too hot.

To do so, they use cool water. Worker bees let the cool water **evaporate**. Then they flap their wings. That spreads the cool air. Workers also do small repairs on broken areas of the nest. They clean up around the nest, too.

When worker bees get older, their tasks change once again. The new tasks are harder. The bees move away from the center of the nest. They go toward the nest's edges. In those areas, the bees make wax.

**Bees build parts of their nests with many little hexagons of wax.**

They use this wax to build new cells. Bees also store food in the nest's outer areas.

Chapter 4

# Work in the Wild

The most dangerous tasks happen when worker bees are older. They must go outside of the nest. One of the most important jobs is **foraging**. The bees need to gather food for the whole colony.

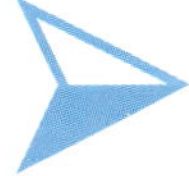

Bees have pouches on their back legs. That helps them collect more pollen.

Each forager bee has its own job. For honeybees, some foragers collect nectar. Bees in the colony use it to make honey. Other foragers collect pollen. To get enough, foragers may visit thousands of flowers every day.

Bees might collect other things, too. For example, some get water. Others might collect twigs and leaves to add to homes.

Sometimes bees may face danger. When that happens, the bees might

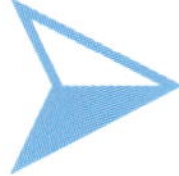
**Bees suck water into their bodies to store it. At their nest, they spit it back out.**

need to fight. They try to protect the colony and the queen.

Sometimes large groups of bees spend time outside together. That is called **swarming**. Bees do this when they need to start a new nest. Swarming takes cooperation.

**A swarm can include thousands of bees.**

The bees fly together. Sometimes, they join up and hang from a tree. The shape moves and shifts. While swarming, some bees go out. They look for spots for a new nest. When a spot is found, the bees move. They start building.

After their hard work, older bees die. They often die away from the nest. That way, other bees don't have to clean up. Just like all their actions, the bees do it for the good of the colony.

**A queen bee can live for five years. Most workers live for about six weeks.**

## FOCUS ON

# Bee Colonies

*Write your answers on a separate piece of paper.*

1. Write a few sentences explaining the role of the queen bee.
2. Do you think queens, drones, or workers have the hardest job? Why?
3. What is one way bees communicate?
   - A. by eating
   - B. by moving
   - C. by cleaning
4. Why might bees need to move to a new nest?
   - A. the old one is too ugly
   - B. the queen doesn't like the old one
   - C. the old nest is not big enough

5. What does **protect** mean in this book?

*Sometimes bees may face danger. When that happens, the bees might need to fight. They try to* ***protect*** *the colony and the queen.*

- A. keep something safe
- B. kill something
- C. run away

6. What does **cooperation** mean in this book?

*Swarming takes* ***cooperation****. The bees fly together. Sometimes, they join up and hang from a tree.*

- A. fighting
- B. building cells
- C. working together

*Answer key on page 32.*

# Glossary

**colonies**
Groups of animals that live together.

**evaporate**
To change from a liquid to a gas.

**foraging**
Searching for food.

**larvae**
Insects that have hatched from eggs and are in the early stages of life.

**mate**
To come together in order to have babies.

**pheromones**
Smells that animals make that affect the behavior of others.

**pollen**
A fine powder produced by some plants that helps create new plants.

**reproduce**
To make new life.

**social**
Likely to spend time with other animals of the same type.

**swarming**
Flying together in a large group.

# To Learn More

## BOOKS

Bassier, Emma. *Bees*. Minneapolis: Abdo Publishing, 2020.

Murray, Laura K. *Why Do We Need Bees?* North Mankato, MN: Capstone Press, 2024.

Sang, Maivboon. *Bee Queens: Rulers of the Hive.* North Mankato, MN: Capstone Press, 2020.

## NOTE TO EDUCATORS

Visit **www.focusreaders.com** to find lesson plans, activities, links, and other resources related to this title.

# Index



**Answer Key: 1.** Answers will vary; **2.** Answers will vary; **3.** B; **4.** C; **5.** A; **6.** C